# wise words

# wise words

## inspiring lessons about life

### edited by jo ryan

Published in the United States in 2004
by Tangent Publications
an imprint of
Axis Publishing Limited
8c Accommodation Road
London NW11 8ED
www.axispublishing.co.uk

Creative Director : Siân Keogh
Managing Editor: Anne Yelland
Production Manager: Toby Reynolds

© 2004 Axis Publishing Limited

ISBN 1-904707-15-7

2 4 6 8 10 9 7 5 3

Printed and bound in China

# about this book

*Wise Words* brings together an inspirational selection of powerful and life-affirming phrases that have in one way or another helped people to live their lives, and combines them with evocative and gently amusing animal photographs that bring out the full humor and pathos of the human condition.

We all get upset by life's irritations at some point and lose our motivation, temper, or sense of humor (sometimes all three at once!). These inspiring examples of wit and wisdom, written by real people based on their real-life experiences, enable us to regain our sense of perspective and rediscover our love of life. As one of the entries so aptly puts it—every moment in time contains the seeds of happiness.

So don't waste a moment!

# about the author

Jo Ryan is an editor and author who has been involved in publishing books and magazines across a wide variety of subjects for many years. From the many hundreds of contributions that were sent to her, she has selected the ones that best sum up what life is all about—our relationships, our ambitions, and our personal well-being.

People need people.

# Strangers are just friends waiting to happen.

Be open to the possibility of
forming friendships, even when
you least expect to.

Love deeply and passionately…

…you might get hurt but it's the only way to live life completely.

Don't settle for being an average person—each of us is extraordinary.

I am still an
individual
when I am with
someone.

No one is easy
to live with all
of the time.

# Go with the flow.

Remember to put you first.

I am free to go,
so I stay.

Friends may come
and go, but
enemies
accumulate.

# Don't let a little dispute injure a great friendship.

Pride can easily blow small
matters out of all proportion.
Get some perspective and
remember what's important.

# Patience is never more important…

# …than when you are on the verge of losing it.

Try to be aware of your mood changing and
your patience slipping—it could save you
from saying something you regret.

The best cure
for a short temper
is a long walk.

Anyone who doesn't think there are two sides to an argument...

...is probably in one.

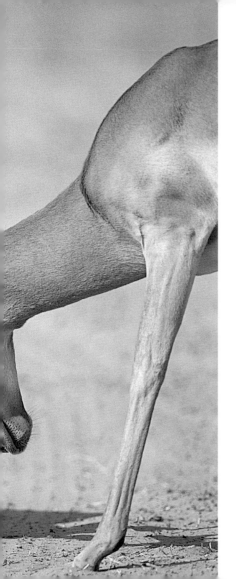

A fight is a great way to clear the air.

A loving
atmosphere is so
important—do all
you can to create
a tranquil,
harmonious home.

I try to think of the things I
missed in my home, and make sure
they are there for my kids.

# Love is unconditional.

Your family is your rock.

All things
grow with love.

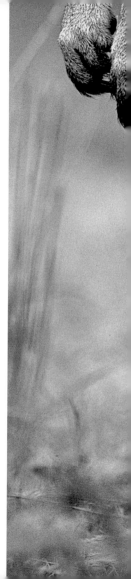

God could not be everywhere—therefore he made mothers.

So remember her birthday!

Share your knowledge with your children—it's one way to achieve immortality.

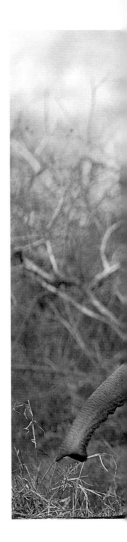

# Kids are naturally curious.

Weren't you? So don't get angry if
accidents result; it's all in
innocence.

# Let kids be kids.

And don't punish them for it,
they only get one chance.

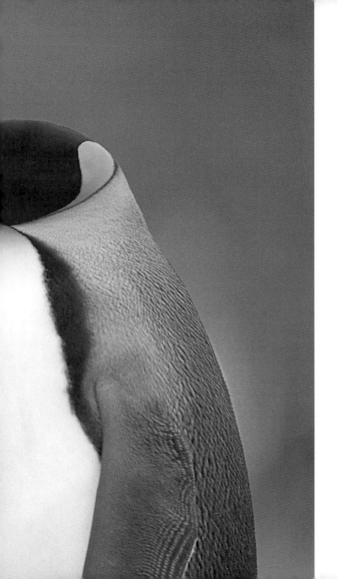

Don't judge
people
by their
relatives.

The most important relationship
in my life is the one with myself.

Better to ask the way than go astray.

The art of good
leadership is to
consider
everyone's opinion
but to make up
your own mind.

Everyone has an opinion, but you
have to make the final decision.

Look at how far you've come, not
at how far you still have to go.

Distance clarifies
everything.

It's alright letting
yourself go, as
long as you can
get yourself back.

Once a year, go someplace you've never been before.

# Open your arms to change, but don't let go of your values.

Being flexible and taking opportunities when they come your way isn't the same as being mercenary with your principles.

# Negative thoughts are a waste of precious energy.

Don't undermine yourself—it's hard enough trying to be happy, even when your mind is on your side.

Nothing is ever
as good or as bad
as it may seem.

Most things don't matter that much in
the long term, so chill out a bit!

Whether you think
you can, or you
think you can't…

…you'll be right
both ways.

Self-belief is all that really matters—
you can do it if you want to.

Don't be afraid of adversity—you may well be surprised by what you can do.

It's OK to come up against obstacles. It is only by rising to a challenge that you find out what you are capable of.

Good judgment comes from bad experiences…

…and a lot of those are caused by bad judgment.

Life is a learning process, and you can never be right all the time.

Experience is a
wonderful thing…

…it enables you
to recognize a
mistake when
you make it again.

I don't always learn from my
mistakes, but I try not to let this
get me down!

No one is good at everything, but everyone is good at something.

If you've got kids, make sure they know what it is that they do well, and help bring out these skills.

# Let your virtues speak for themselves.

Very important for your well-being I think—
walk the walk, don't just talk the talk.

Let people feel the weight of who you are, and let them deal with it.

A man is successful if he gets up in the morning…

…goes to bed at night, and in between does what he wants to do.

We should all be free to do what most inspires us and feel good about living that way.

# Go easy on yourself—you can only take so much.

It's foolish to drive yourself to an early grave working too hard—remember to enjoy life as you travel through it.

A snooze
button is a
poor substitute
for no alarm
clock at all.

If I have the option, I sleep.

# The early bird gets the worm, but the second mouse gets the cheese.

Sometimes there are good
reasons not to blindly rush in, but
let others lead the way instead.

Slow and steady
wins the race.

The other line always
moves faster until you join it.

Everything comes
to those who wait.

Kings and their
realms pass away,
but time goes
on forever.

# Every moment in time contains the seeds of happiness.

I've learned that I can screw up the good times in my life if I'm not focused on the right things, being true to myself and enjoying without strings attached.

Lead me not into temptation
(I can find the way myself).

The end of one thing is merely
the beginning of another.

Worrying never
changed anything.

When a pessimist has
nothing to worry about…

…he worries about why he has
nothing to worry about.

Don't get into a negative mind-
set—enjoy a happy, worry-free
period while it lasts.

# Snap out of it, and pull yourself together.

Sometimes I just have to remember this and it gets me motivated again.

# Cheer up! Remember, the less you have, the more there is to get.

I get depressed when I look at things in a negative way.

# Fear always springs from ignorance.

I try to remember that I am mostly afraid
of the situations I am most ignorant of,
so there's an easy solution—learn!

If you can stay calm while all around you is chaos…

…then you probably haven't completely understood the seriousness of the situation.

Sometimes it is better to stand back from a
difficult situation and not take it too seriously.
You are far more likely to find a solution this
way than going into a panic.

Generally speaking, you aren't learning much when your mouth is moving.

Unless you're learning a language.
Otherwise, try to listen a bit more.

Wonder is the beginning of wisdom.

True wisdom is
to live in the present,
plan for the future, and
profit from the past.

Imagination is stronger
than knowledge…

…dreams are more
powerful than facts, and
hope can triumph over
experience.

Whatever setbacks you
encounter, don't give up on your
hopes and dreams.

# Faith begins where reason ends.

We reach a point where it's not enough to know something, we have to be willing to step out in faith and start our real journey.

Listen to the silence.

Life—it's nothing like the brochure.